Michigan's Leelanau County

©1988 by Ken Scott. All rights reserved. No part of this book may be reproduced in any form or by any means without permission in writing from the author.
Library of Congress catalog card number 88-091098

Printed and bound by
The Hamblin Company
109 E. Logan St.
Tecumseh, Michigan 49286
517-423-7491

First edition 1988
Second edition 1989
Designed by Paul Montie and Fritz Klaetke, Visual Dialogue.

Published and distributed by
Peninsula Publishing
P.O. Box 668
Suttons Bay, MI 49682
616-271-6070

Enlargements, some in limited editions, of the photographs in this book can be ordered by writing Ken Scott, c/o the publisher. Please address questions and comments to the publisher.

MICHIGAN'S
LEELANAU COUNTY

> 9.-3-1991, USA, MI
>
> Ein kleines Willkommensgeschenk, damit Ihr schon einen kleinen Vorgeschmack bekommt, bevor es auf große Reise geht.
> Freue mich riesig, daß Ihr hier seit, endlich nach 8 Monaten ein Wiedersehen.
> Love
> Silke

a collection of photographs by

KEN SCOTT

To my parents, Larry and Ann Scott,
who gave me the support to grow.
To Alice and Trevor,
who make growth meaningful.

Jutting thirty miles into Lake Michigan, the Leelanau Peninsula is an unique environment surpassed by few places in the world. Water — the many inland lakes and the nearly 100 miles of coast line — defines its character; from most hills one can see water glistening in the sun. Continually shaped by wind and sand, water and ice, this is a geologically young landscape, beguiling in its serenity, its rolling hills, blue lakes and white beaches, its forests of beech, maple and birch. Yet when storms howl off the lake it can be frightening: in summer thunderstorms pack wind and hail, waves undercut the bluffs, sand stings through the air, in winter blizzards isolate it from the rest of the world. This peninsular isolation insures the county's character, it is a place to which one comes and from which one returns, not a point one passes through going some place else. Leelanau is a destination of hills and water, light and weather. It is a land where each season is distinct, each hour unique, where the forests flash from pastel to flame in six months, where the sun sets into the lake and the lake catches fire. Here water generates the weather; in winter cold air crossing the lake blankets the county in snow; in summer the lakes respire a refreshing cool; the water ripens the fruit that comes by the ton from the orchards, vineyards, and fields that grace the hills; the water; the water beckons people to swim, sail, to fish and ski. It is a place where the play of light on leaf and flower, on sand and water, inspires, where that inspiration carries one through days in a more frenzied world. Leelanau is a land of many places, of bluffs, dunes, beaches, of small towns and farms among the forests. Each is a place to turn to, to return to, to express the body's energy, to reflect and contemplate. Leelanau is to explore.

DUNCAN MORAN
Lake Leelanau

Rest Time

Harbor Light

An Autumn Mood

Along-Shore

Harvest Motif

Colors of Summer

An Orchard View

Tarts

8

Rural Passageway

Showey Lady's Show Their Slippers

Witness to a Marvel

A Head Above the Rest

South Manitou Lighthouse

Family

About to Burst

D. H. Day Farm

Color Tour

Of Bluffs, Bays and Lakes

Detail of an Alberta Clipper

Snowbird III

Bearberry

The Bear, She Lives

Lakelandscape

N.J.'s

The Art of Shoreline Erosion

A Reflective Victoria

Malabar

The Moon Room

Stone, Wood, Water

Cumulomammatus

Dance of the Dune

The Bear, She Watches

Salmon Run

Columbine

A Moving Scene

Swamily

Misty Morn II

Snowscape

Heading Home

Ahh ... The Crystal

A Farm for Cherries

Old and New

A Bicentennial Memento

Barnyard With Character

A Fine Fall Day

Detail of a Lake Michigan Sunset II

New Beginnings

Shadowplay

Morning Calm

Sleeping Bear Coast Guard Station

Sunset Promenade

A Lunar Eve

The Bear, She Sleeps

A View to Remember

Red Barrel in "The Narrows"

Red Barrel in "The Narrows" III

Falls Approach

Prelude to Winter

Two Swans, Too Cold, To Pose

Moonrise II

A Reflective Refueling

Passage

Iced

10 Painters Painting

A Splash of Winter

Moonlit Hearth

Dunescape

Gull Isle

Glazed

An Evening Silhouette

Grand Traverse Lighthouse

Lilies by the Wall

Marina Storm

A Point from Above

The Family that Farms Together ...

Spring Blossom

Moon over Maples

A Loyal Lot

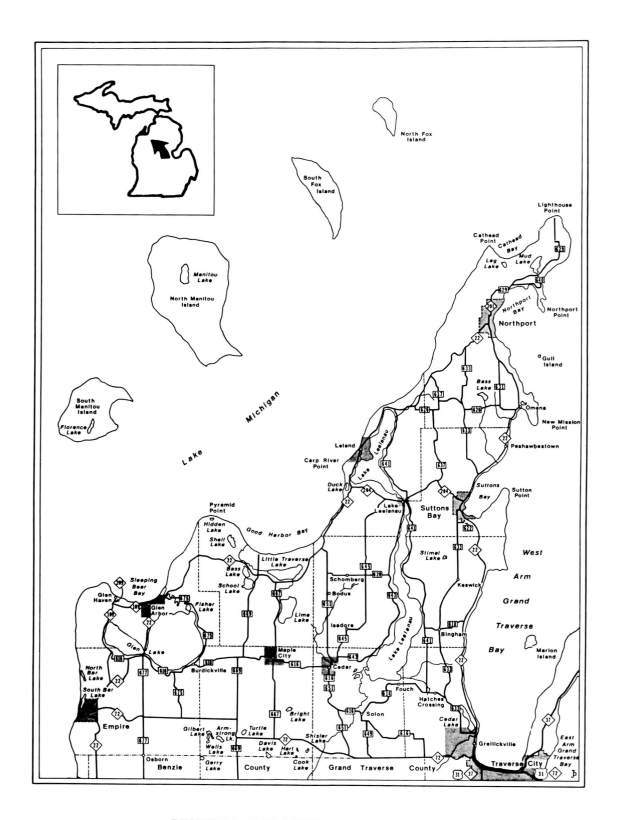

GENERAL MAP OF LEELANAU COUNTY

Map courtesy of the Leelanau County Planning Department

GUIDE TO PLATES

1 Leland's Fishtown
2 Leland
3 Good Harbor Bay shoreline
4 Shoreline along East 22
5 Cutting hay along 645
6 Wheat along 204
7 One of many cherry farms in the county
8 Close up of tart cherries
9 One of many scenic back roads around the county
10 Showy lady's slippers
11 View from Gill's Pier area
12 Sunflowers near cedar
13 View of the light house from Sleeping Bear Dunes
14 One family's summation of their visit to the county
15 A spring bud on the dunes
16 Along 109
17 Cedar - Maple City area
18 Aerial view of Carp River Pt. - N. Lake Leelanau - Duck Lake
19 On Sleeping Bear Bay shore looking towards Sleeping Bear Point
20 A 1946 Aeronca Chief on N. Lake Leelanau
21 A spring bloom on the Dunes
22 View in Devils Hole area of the Dunes
23 View of Little Traverse Lake, Good Harbor Bay and Pyramid Pt.
24 The heart of Lake Leelanau the village
25 Detail of Sleeping Bear Bay shoreline
26 Bridge over the Victoria Creek in Cedar
27 An overnight visit to Suttons Bay Marina
28 Outhouse along East 22
29 St. Mary's school and church in Lake Leelenau the village
30 A cloud formation with all the makings for a tornado
31 Dune grass on the Dunes
32 Ice fishing on Little Glen Lake
33 A scene along east 22
34 Found in the woods around the County
35 A lining is laid at Glen's Landfill along 72
36 A swan family on Lake Leelanau
37 Suttons Bay Moorings
38 A scene along 633
39 Aerial view of Glen Lakes at sunset
40 Part of the Crystal River at day break
41 Cherry orchard north of Suttons Bay
42 Just south of Northport
43 Along West 22 near Little Traverse Lake
44 Along West 22
45 Shoreline along East 22 near Peshawbestown
46 Bow of the Mishe-Mokwa in Leland's harbor
47 Cemetery on 626
48 A spectacle that happens in May along East 22
49 Suttons Bay Marina
50 During the Alberta Clipper of Feb 87
51 Along Sleeping Bear Bay
52 Scene over the county
53 Aerial view of Sleeping Bear Dune
54 Empire Bluffs overlook of S. Bar Lake, The Dunes and Manitou Islands
55 View from bridge on 204 in Lake Leelanau
56 Same view
57 Cedar area
58 A December morning
59 The Narrows, Lake Leelanau
60 Aerial view of Sleeping Bear Point, Bay and the Glen Lakes
61 Greilickville
62 The passage light and North Manitou Island
63 Along East 22
64 The old mill on Belanger Pond
65 The Dunes from Empire
66 Time exposed star trails over Author's home
67 Sleeping Bear Dune
68 Bellow Island SE of Northport
69 Indian Mission Church on West 22 south of Northport
70 An evening along 633
71 Just prior to reopening as Museum for the public
72 Old house along 72
73 Charter boats in Leland
74 Aerial view of Pyramid Point
75 The Jughead family near Northport
76 Old farm in the Dunes Area
77 Along East 22
78 A scene in the Maple City area, but felt around the county

Ken Scott is a self taught photographer who lives with his wife and son in Leelanau County. He works exclusively with a 35 mm camera, two lenses, a tripod and Kodachrome film, striving to realize his vision without gadgetry. He participates in Art fairs and exhibits in galleries throughout Michigan, winning awards in each, and is a member of several regional art associations: The Glen Lake Artists' Association, Northern Michigan Artists and Craftsmen, and the Traverse City Arts Council.